MW00977788

GRACE
TO SEE

GRACE TO SEE

Living with the Enemy:
My Story of Survival

ELISABETH WOMBLE

XULON PRESS

Xulon Press
2301 Lucien Way #415
Maitland, FL 32751
407.339.4217
www.xulonpress.com

© 2020 by ELISABETH WOMBLE

All rights reserved solely by the author. The author guarantees all
contents are original and do not infringe upon the legal rights of
any other person or work. No part of this book may be reproduced
in any form without the permission of the author. The views
expressed in this book are not necessarily those of the publisher.

Unless otherwise indicated, Scripture taken from the New King
James Version®. Copyright © 1982 by Thomas Nelson. Used by
permission. All rights reserved.

Painting on front of book by: Jennifer Kenney. Used by permission.
All rights reserved.

Author's Coach: Jacqueline Arnold, www.sweetlifeusa.com

Printed in the United States of America.

Paperback ISBN-13: 978-1-63221-981-7
eBook ISBN-13: 978-1-6322-1982-4

DEDICATION

I dedicate this book to my precious, beautiful
daughter, Jessica.

Wow, what a journey we have been on together!
Always remember

You truly are More than a Conqueror,
and will always be my Sweetie!

He will cover you with his
feathers, and under his
wings you will find refuge;
his faithfulness will be your
shield and rampart. PSALM 91:4

Acknowledgments

First and foremost, I want to thank my precious Savior and Lord, Jesus Christ. Thank You for saving my life, and showing me how to truly live and have abundant life through You.

Thank you to my husband, Steve Womble. Thank you for supporting me through every step of the way in following my dream to write this book. Thank you for making this possible, and believing in me. I love you!

Thank you to my daughter, Jessica. Thank you for encouraging me, and telling me you are proud of me through this whole process. Thank you also for believing in me. I am **so** thankful God chose me to be your mom, and you are truly one of my best friends! I love you to the moon and back sweetie!

Thank you to my sweet Touching Hearts sisters. Thank you for standing by me, and journeying with me these last fifteen years. Thank you for teaching me how to truly worship and find freedom. Martha Wilson, thank you for the many times you reminded me to stay in **today**, and for being my dear friend and mentor! I love you, and carry you in my heart!

Thank you to my friend and pen pal, Dawn Smith Jordan. Thank you for being such a great example to me as I have watched your life since I was a teenager. You will never know how much you mean to me, thank you for teaching me to always Keep Believing!

Thank you to my sweet friend, Debbie Gronner. Thank you so much for your constant encouragement and letting me use you as my sounding board through this process. You are precious, and I treasure our friendship!

Thank you to "my angel," Jennifer Kenney. Thank you for the many different prophetic paintings and letting me use one of them as the cover of this book. This painting represents to me the transformation that God has done and is doing in me! You are so talented! Thank you for being such a great friend and second momma to me! I love you!

Thank you to my other second mommas, Peggy Dobbs and Kathie Sipple, for loving me, and praying me through and fighting for me through many difficult times. I love you both so much!

Thank you to my family and friends, who are too many to name individually. Thank you for being there for me, and encouraging me to tell my story.

Thank you to my sweet author coach, Jacqueline Arnold. Thank you for your insights, encouragement, and believing in me.

TABLE OF CONTENTS

INTRODUCTION

Storms of life can be devastating and earth-shattering. My life has been filled with many different storms that almost took me out. Key word there is **almost**! Praise the Lord, what Satan meant for evil, God has turned around to be used for His glory! Through life experiences and learning how to have a true intimate relationship with Jesus Christ, He has taught me how to overcome and have victory. I pray the same for you in your life, and that as you read my story God will teach you some strategies to fight against the enemy, heal your heart, and bring you closer to Him! We can go from **victims** to **victors**. He can turn the ashes of our life into something beautiful for Him, and turn **tragedy** into **triumph**. What seems like a total mess in our lives can be changed to a message of hope for others.

As I write this book, please remember that this is written from my perception of events that happened in my life. Others may see things differently, but I am writing from my heart, events and circumstances that God allowed to happen to me. Also, as I write this book, some of the actual names of people will be changed. I will also not be going into great detail about different traumatic events, but give you enough to see and feel what I have been through. The details aren't important, but the ultimate message of hope, peace, His love, and true joy are important!

I pray that in each chapter you will see that God has given me *Grace to See* a different attribute of Him through the different events of my life. It is amazing to me how God is our **everything**, and how He truly knows and cares about every detail of our lives, and shows Himself in many different ways. Maybe you don't feel that way right now, and your life is falling apart. I pray that God will use my story to encourage you, and give you hope.

One of my favorite passages of scripture that I cling to is Psalm 61:2-4:

> *From the end of the earth I will cry to You.*
> *When my heart is overwhelmed; Lead me to*
> *the Rock that is higher than I. For you have*
> *been a shelter for me, a strong tower from then*
> *enemy. I will abide in the shelter of your wings.*

Hallelujah! He can handle it when we are overwhelmed, and we can trust His heart for us. Yes, Satan is out to destroy us, and make us give up. I pray as you read the journey of my life and see the strategies God has given me to fight the enemy, it will help you in your life. Please open your heart, drop your doubts, and go on this journey with me...maybe, just maybe, you will see that if God can bring me through everything I have been through, He can and will bring you through too!

CHAPTER ONE

MOMMY, WHERE ARE YOU?

GOD AS MY ABBA DADDY

Psalm 27:10 - *"When my father and mother forsake me, Then the Lord will take care of me"*

ONE MORNING IN 1982 WHEN I WAS FIVE YEARS OLD, my brother Daniel was three, and my brother Mark was one year old, our biological father picked us up from the babysitter's house. The night before he had beaten our mom up really bad again, and she was in the hospital. I will never forget when he picked us up how he just said in a regular voice, "Your mom died today, and we are moving to Kentucky!" He wasn't upset or anything and we weren't supposed to talk about our mom.

I really don't know how long we were in Kentucky. I do know it was long enough for my dad to continue molesting me and eventually raping me several times. I didn't know until several years later that what he did to me was wrong and called incest and rape.

One afternoon, a policeman knocked on our door, and I remember hearing him say, "Charles Raider, if you don't get your children back down to Georgia within twenty-four hours, you will be going to jail!"

So, he loaded the car back up and took us back to Georgia. We went inside the church we used to go to, and all of the sudden we see our **mom**! Wait, wasn't she supposed to be dead? I remember being so confused and scared.

Before Charles kidnapped us, our house was very chaotic and noisy. My dad was very mean and abusive in every way. He would do crazy stuff if he got mad at my mom, like dump us off the couch we were sitting on, go around the house screaming, and beating on the walls with the radio blaring loud. My brother, Daniel, and I used to be terrified of airplanes, because it reminded us of how loud it was in our house. We saw our mom get thrown around and beat up a lot. She had already had a terrible childhood of abuse, and she ended up staying with our dad for seven years of hell!

After he brought us back from when he kidnapped us, my mom filed for divorce, and we never heard from our dad again until I was an adult. My mom worked a full-time job at a law firm, and she was a single mom now to three terrified kids. We didn't have much at all, not even a car for a long time. We walked everywhere, and sometimes slept on the church bus. Then one of the mean deacons of the church found out and kicked us off the bus, and we had to go live with my mom's parents for a while. (The same ones who abused my mom and her siblings terribly, all the way until my mom left for Bible college). The church eventually let us live in a home for unwed mothers, but we all shared one full-size mattress for a while, and didn't have much food. My brother, Daniel, and I made ourselves very sick eating a whole jar of mayonnaise because we were so hungry. It took a very long time for either of us to touch mayonnaise again!

My mom did the best she could with what she had. I know that now as an adult, but I didn't understand it as a little girl. We lived pretty much from cut-off to cut-off on the power, water, and gas bills. I remember many times hearing my mom calling the utility offices, begging them to turn the power, gas, or water back on. I remember freezing a lot because we didn't have heat. My mom would open the oven door and we would all stand in front of it and try to get warm. I always wondered why my mom tithed her last bit of money to the church, knowing that she would just have to ask for it back, because we didn't have enough food, or gas for the car we eventually got.

Our mom was also dealing with major depression that affected our lives greatly. You will learn more about that in the next chapter. I was very young, but I pretty much took care of my brothers and was like a mom to them. I was very protective of them, and wanted to make sure they were okay. I still do to this day.

Mom struggled so much, but as an adult now myself, I know she did her best, especially after everything she had been through. My mom's depression was severe, and for some reason she always felt guilty for taking medicine for depression. The church we went to made her feel like it was a sin for Christians to rely on medicine. Oh my goodness, they have no idea the mistake they made in telling her that, and what havoc it caused in our lives! So many times, she would tell us she wanted to die, and that she wasn't a good mom. We watched the cycle of depression unravel until she ended up in a mental institute several times.

I remember being scared all the time that I was going to find my mom dead from suicide. At eight years old, I carried a very heavy burden of worrying about my mom's bills, if we would have enough to eat, would she be alive the next day, would she come back from her trips to get "coffee," would she talk to us when she came home from work or go upstairs and go straight to bed? I didn't have much of a childhood. I always felt like I was born an adult.

This started to develop anger in me as a young girl, plus not having a dad. I hadn't even told my mom yet what

Charles, my dad did to me, because I didn't even know it was wrong until I was in fourth grade health class. There we learned about the birds and the bees, and appropriate and inappropriate touching.

Unfortunately, when children are sexually abused, it makes them feel like targets. I would learn later in life that is truly what the enemy (Satan) does to us as survivors: makes us feel like and look like weak targets. I ended up being molested by another daycare worker while my mom was at work. Then when I was a teenager, I believe summer of sixth grade, one of our neighbors, Roy, molested me. He was this older man who tried to be nice to us and taught Daniel and Mark karate. One day I got off the school bus, and he came and gave me a hug and said I could call him "daddy." I remember then starting to feel very creepy around him. That weekend, something was wrong with his car, and he asked my mom if I could ride to the store with him, and she said yes. We went down the road, and he started rubbing me up high on my legs, my back, and running his hands through my hair. I jerked away from him and told him to stop. He hit me really hard, and I don't remember what all he did to me. I just know that when we got home, I felt disgusting. He got out of the car and kissed my mom in the lips and thanked her for letting me go. My mom knew something was wrong and she was disgusted with him. I stayed in my room for a week and wouldn't talk about it.

This was when I started really feeling like something was wrong with me, because all these men wanted to hurt me. I became very paranoid and afraid of almost all men, and I started really hating myself. I started questioning God, and if He really loved me like I had always heard He did. I wondered what I did to make God not love me, and so many bad things continue to happen to me. I had this huge dad-sized, God-sized void in my heart that just continued to grow with bitterness and anger for a long time.

As an adult, I was attacked again! I was already married, and a lot had happened, as you will learn in later chapters. By this time, my mom and I ended up working at the same law firm in Atlanta, and we would ride Marta together a lot. Well, this one terrible afternoon, the train was crammed full of people, seriously, like sardines. Somehow, I ended up right in the middle of four black men. I was already feeling uncomfortable before anything happened. I couldn't turn and didn't have anything to hold onto, except for the bar above me. I could see my mom across the aisle, and she knew something was wrong. When the train started moving, the man behind me started rubbing himself all up and down my butt, and rubbing all over me. I was jabbing him as much as I could with my elbow. The other men around me were saying crude things to me. I had tears just rolling down my face, and my mom was mouthing to me, "I'm sorry!" It felt like this went on for eternity before we finally got to our stop.

This triggered so many emotions for me and brought back so many different fears, bad memories and shame in me. I was traumatized yet again and had to take a week off work to get myself back together again. I didn't ride Marta for a long time after that. Of course, we didn't know who the men were, so we couldn't really report anything. Again, this did a number on my self-esteem and my relationship with God.

Chapter Two

Trashbags and Starvation

God as my Savior

Joshua 1:9 – *"Have I not commanded you? Be strong and of good courage; do not be afraid, nor be dismayed, for the Lord your God is with you wherever you go."*

MOM STRUGGLED WITH SEVERE DEPRESSION FOR most of my life. She had a terrible childhood, and then married my abusive father and did the best she could to take care of us three kids. Unfortunately, she just needed more help than anyone could give her. She went in and out of mental institutes/hospitals from the time I was six years old until I was around thirteen years old. Sometimes she would be gone for a couple of weeks, and then come back home. Other times it was a few months at a time.

For a long time, our church passed Daniel, Mark, and me around to different homes, trying to keep us out of the foster care system. We would come home and hope things would be better this time, but that hope always came to an end very quickly. Then, "Here we go again, Mom is back in the hospital, and we are going to someone else's home."

I became like the mother to Daniel and Mark. I tried to take care of them the best I could, helping with homework, trying to do what an eight-year-old could do around the house, play with them, anything I could do to keep them safe and their minds off of the reality we really lived in. As mentioned earlier, we never knew when our water, power, or gas was going to be turned off, or if Mom would have money to get enough food. I would make sure the house was cleaned, and then try to scrounge up any change that was in the couch or in Mom's purse, to see if we could go to McDonald's to eat.

Things got to such a bad point with mom, she didn't want to get out of bed at all to go to work or do anything. People at the church got tired of helping and someone called DFACS. When they came and saw the condition of our home, and saw how depressed Mom was they took us away and put us in the Friday Home in Fayetteville. We were there for at least a year while Mom went to the hospital and got counseling again. Then we all came back home. For a while, things were okay.

I was around ten years old and helping Mom with her finances, trying to not have any utilities cut off. I wanted so badly to take care of my mom, my brothers, the house, our schoolwork, everything but me. I didn't even know how to be a normal little girl. Then when I was eleven and learned about sex education and what was right and wrong with people touching in private areas, the light bulb went off. I understood all the horrible things that my dad did to me were **wrong**, and I didn't deserve that. I realized for the first time I was a victim of incest and rape. How in the world could I tell my mom? I told an adult in my youth group, and she helped me tell my mom. It didn't go over very good and so many questions came up.

From that time on, things were never the same. I saw the way she looked at me with doubt and always asking a thousand questions. Then I guess some details rang true to her and after the doctor confirmed that I had been raped, she believed me. Mom went into a downward spiral, and the whole cycle of depression started again. She told us what a bad mom she was and how she didn't deserve to live, etc.

Then one day when I was eleven years old, Mom said she needed to go for a drive and get some coffee and would be back. I knew in my heart something was very wrong. The hours went by, and I was running out of things to do to keep Daniel and Mark busy and not realize that Mom wasn't home yet. We were hungry and I found something to feed us. It was getting dark and still our mom wasn't home. Then there was a knock at the door. Our social worker from DFACS came in and had three trash bags in her hand. She told us our mom had to go back to the hospital and we were going to foster homes.

She said, "Here's you a bag, you a bag, and you a bag, go pack some clothes and a few things you want we have to go." There was no sympathy or real explanation and I was so confused, hurt, and mad. Then we got in her car and she broke the worst news ever: "Elisabeth, you are going to a foster home in Fayetteville, and Daniel and Mark are going back to the Friday Home in Fayetteville. They don't have enough room for another girl."

My heart sank to my stomach. This was the first time I was separated from my brothers whom I loved so much. Little did I know, that would be the last time we would live together again until I was eighteen years old. I went to the home of a couple in our church. I always thought this couple was weird, but I had no idea just how weird they were, and to my surprise, how mean the mom was. I lived in this home for six months, and could only have salad, apple juice and water. The lady thought I was fat, and I wasn't that big at all at eleven years old! I shared a room with a baby who was in a body cast, that I couldn't touch. All I could do was sing to her. The man of the house never did anything to stand up for me or help me. I had to clean all the time. I was **starving**! Now, how was I going to get out of here and how could I make someone at church believe me?

This lady had people watching me at school, and if one of my friends bought me a real lunch, she knew about it when I got home, and then I couldn't eat anything for dinner. She made me this shake to have for my lunches. My grades started to drop, I was very tired all the time, shaking all the time, and emotionally not doing well. I blamed myself for ever telling my mom anything about my dad. I blamed myself for Daniel and Mark having to go to the other home, and I am stuck in Hell!

Thankfully, while this was going on, I was writing in my journal at school in my English class. Part of my journal was about not having a dad; the other part was about everything this lady was doing to me. I can never thank Mr. Fitch and Mrs. Bryant enough for saving my life. Mrs. Bryant knew something was wrong with me, and was very nice to me, and helped me make it through this time.

Mr. Fitch was my English teacher. He came to me one day and said, "Do you care if I publish this in the newspaper?" He pointed to what I had written about not having a dad.

I said, "No, I don't care."

When I came to school the next day, there were a lot of police there and I had no idea what was going on. Well, they were there for **me**! Mr. Fitch had published all the journal entries I had written about this lady starving me, and all of the mean things she said to me, in the Fayette County newspaper. Next thing I knew, my social worker picked me up from school and took me to another foster home in Fayetteville. It wasn't too far from my mom's apartment. I thought many times about running away and going to my mom's, but I knew I would get in trouble, and I didn't want to get my mom in trouble either.

This house was one of the good homes. I could eat whatever I wanted and as much as I wanted. I started hoarding my food, and swore to myself I would never be that hungry again. At this house I shared a room with another girl named Kerri. My foster parents here also had a baby boy who was a crack baby. This baby cried all the time! We had to take turns taking care of him through the night. I got really close to this family and liked being there. I still missed my brothers, though, and only got see them every now and then. I thought this family was going to adopt me, or that was where I would be until my mom got better, or whatever was going to happen.

When I was thirteen, another girl named Kerri was also living with us. So, we had two Kerris, the crack baby, me, the mom and dad and their little girl. I started noticing the mom wasn't happy and had bad mood swings. I didn't let it get to me, because hey, I could still eat, so I was good. One thing led to another, and one day the mom and dad called me and the two Kerri's to the kitchen table. They told us they were getting divorced, and that DFACS was coming in the morning to pick us up. **What?** One of the Kerri's and I went outside and washed their dog and cried and cried. I mean I was there for more than a year, then in one night everything was over!

The next morning my caseworker picked me up and took me to her office. My mom was there. I hadn't seen her in a long time. Daniel and Mark were there, and I hadn't seen them in a long time either. Mom had to make a decision to terminate her rights to us, because she just couldn't take care of us. I felt like she had given up on us, and I was very, very mad and hurt. Then the social worker said we were all three going to the Georgia Baptist Children's Home in Palmetto. I had never heard of Palmetto. I was just glad to be with my brothers.

Well, even though we were all at the same place, we all lived in different cottages. This was when my real depression started. I really didn't care about anything, and really didn't want to live. I wasn't feeling good at all and didn't know why. I finally convinced my cottage parent to take me to the doctor. They did blood work and tests on my stomach. I found out in one day that I had a bleeding ulcer, high cholesterol, and my thyroid was dead. I was fourteen years old! So, I ended up on a bunch of medicine to take care of all of these things. My thyroid took forever to level off, and the doctors were changing my dose all the time. They finally said I pretty much had a physical and chemical breakdown from all the stress in my life. Also, going from starving to being able to eat anything threw my body chemicals off. I could have told them that! So, that was the beginning of a long road dealing with my weight issues, depression, and thyroid problems.

We were at the children's home until I was eighteen years old and graduated from high school. Then all of the sudden, DFACS sent all three of us back home at the same time. We hadn't all lived together in seven years, what were they thinking? I was eighteen, Daniel was sixteen, and Mark was fourteen. We had all been raised the last seven years very differently, and now we were all back under the same roof with our mom. Yes, we were glad to all be back together. However, we all had so many issues and feelings from everything that happened to us, so the new living arrangements didn't go very well.

I think I was home for maybe three months, then I wanted **out**. I made a mistake and moved in with a lady, her boyfriend, and her two little boys. I was the live-in nanny! **Help**, I was eighteen, very traumatized from life, and now I was pretty much the full-time mom of a little baby boy, and a three-year-old. The mom and boyfriend were truck drivers, and gone for two or three weeks at a time, home for a couple of days, and then back on the road. I did this for a year, and in that year I moved with them **five** times! The mom went from man to man to man, and my heart hurt for these little boys so much. I took care of them like they were mine. Finally, when she was going to move on to the sixth man, I had enough and got the nerve to say, "No!" I had to make the choice to go back to my mom's and leave the little boys, which was very hard to do.

So, I went back home for a while and started working at Chick-fil-A. I was nineteen years old at this time. While working there, one of my good friends said, "Hey, I know a guy that I think you would get along real good with. He is a big guy, but he is very nice, do you want me to give him your number?"

I said, "Sure, he probably won't call, but if he does that would be nice."

I didn't think anything of it, and thought, *Yeah, right, I am not going on a blind date.*

Remember: in this book, I have changed some of the names of people to protect the innocent and people who are still alive. That night "Jimmy" did call me, and we talked for four hours. The next day he called me, and wanted to meet me.

Long story short, we dated for a couple of months and then he asked me to marry him. I thought I had been rescued and was going to start this wonderful new life!

CHAPTER THREE

HONEYMOON FAIL

GOD AS MY HOPE

Romans 15:13 – *"Now may the God of hope fill you with all joy and peace in believing, that you may abound in hope by the power of the Holy Spirit."*

APRIL 25, 1997, I GOT MARRIED TO "JIMMY" AT THE courthouse in McDonough, GA. We went away for the weekend for our honeymoon. We never tried to have sex or anything before we got married, and even though I was abused as a child, I saw myself as a virgin. Jimmy was going to be the first person I willingly gave myself to. We were very much in love. He was a gentle teddy bear.

Most people don't know this next part about me, so I am being very vulnerable with you as you read this book.

I want to be real and show others it is okay to be real. I won't go into too much detail, in case a child ever picks up this book to read it. Our honeymoon night was terrible, to say the least. We tried and tried, and I couldn't do it. We gave up that night and said we would try again the next day. I cried and cried, and I could tell Jimmy was very disappointed, even though he tried to be there for me. So, the next day came and we tried and still couldn't fully have sex. I didn't know if I was going crazy or what in the world was wrong with me. We still enjoyed our time together, and then when we came home we had smiles on our faces like our honeymoon was the best, even though I was dying on the inside. I had no one I could really tell that I was a failure in this area of my life.

We tried for six months, and it was just a terrible experience for us both. Finally, I said I needed to go to the doctor to see what was wrong. I didn't know if I was shutting down because of memories from my childhood experiences, or why I couldn't physically fulfill my role as a wife in the right way. Jimmy was very patient. He did get frustrated of course; I think any man would have. I really thought many times Jimmy was going to leave me, but he didn't. So, we went to the OB-GYN. I was terrified. This was the first time I had been to one since I was eleven years old and had to prove to my mom and the detective that I was really raped.

Jimmy was in the room with me, and the doctor started the exam. I hadn't told him anything about my past. The doctor stopped the exam shortly after starting.

He said, "Ma'am, I have a personal and serious question to ask you."

I thought, *Oh no, I have a tumor or something inside me or something preventing me from having sex.*

He said, "Ma'am, have you ever been raped or abused as a child?"

I busted out crying, and said, "**Yes!**" The anger and hurt of all that came back inside me at that moment, as I was so embarrassed.

He said, "No wonder you are having a hard time having sex, I can't even get my little finger inside of you. You are like a little girl inside, and we will need to do surgery."

I was thinking: *What, I have to have surgery to be able to have sex? That is crazy!*

I had never heard of anyone having this problem. What was wrong with me? We went through a process of tests to prepare for the surgery. I finally had surgery, and felt some kind of relief that hopefully that part of my past was over, and now I could be a wife in every way. We had to wait for six more weeks after my surgery to even try to have sex. Finally, after eight months and six weeks of being married Jimmy and I were finally able to have sex. After a while, I was able to enjoy it, and felt like I had finally made Jimmy happy. Our sex life was good for about a year...

Jimmy got hurt at work our second year of marriage. He fell off a catwalk at work, busted his knee up, and couldn't walk for a while. Then he gained a lot of weight, was very depressed, and he was diagnosed with diabetes. The diabetes and depression over time took the joy out of our sex life. During this time, we lost everything and had to live with my mom for a while. It took a long time to get back on our feet again. I worked full-time and went to school at night and got my associate's degree in accounting. Jimmy was never able to go back to work again. The diabetes hit him hard and caused severe neuropathy all over his body. I will tell you more about this time of our life in future chapters.

I was only twenty when we got married, and twenty-two when everything fell apart for us financially (the first time), and diabetes took over Jimmy's life. He didn't take care of himself as he should have and was very depressed. At the same time, I was having a lot of emotional issues from my past. My paranoia got really bad. I was scared to go anywhere by myself and didn't want to be home by myself at all. When we went to bed at night, I had a chair under the doorknob and a baseball bat next to my bed. I was ready to attack someone if they came in and tried to hurt me again.

I didn't get good counseling growing up, and I knew I needed it badly. I had so many different pent-up emotions inside. I sought out some Christian counseling and found a good counselor to help me work through my childhood memories. It took a while, but I was able to get to the point of true forgiveness toward my mom, my dad, the foster home system, the man who molested me as a teenager, and so many other things in my life. I felt free for the first time and I wanted to find my biological father and tell him I forgave him. I hadn't seen him since I was five or six years old. I will tell you about this in the next chapter.

In this chapter, I said I saw God as my hope. He is my hope, my only hope. He is your only hope too, even if you don't realize it yet. You see I was at the end of myself when I thought I wasn't going to be able to be a good wife. It devastated me! Without God in my life, I believe I would have given up at this point. I thank God for giving me the hope to continue.

Chapter Four

Facing the Giant Leads to Forgiveness

God's kind of forgiveness

Philippians 4:13 – *"I can do all things through Christ who strengthens me."*

FORGIVENESS IS A POWERFUL WORD AND A POWerful attribute God wants us to have. I carried so much bitterness, anger, and pure hatred in my heart for so long, I didn't know how to live without all that in me. When God helped me forgive my mom, the foster care system, the men who hurt me, and filled me with His peace, joy, and compassion, I didn't really know how to live in that freedom. There was still one person I had forgiven, but toward whom I still carried a lot of hurt and disappointment ...my biological father!

When I was twenty-one, I started having this longing to find my biological father, to let him know I forgave him for everything, and I wanted to tell him to his face. I hadn't seen my dad since I was six years old and lived most of my life hating him. Really even beyond that, as a teenager I had planned out how I was going to kill him and make him pay for everything he did to me, my mom, and our family. One thing I learned about forgiveness was that it didn't mean what happened, or what someone did to you was okay, or that you even had to have a relationship with them again. It meant you truly forgave them from your heart, and released them from trying to make them pay.

Really, all of that anger was killing me. I know I have heard it said that un-forgiveness is like drinking poison, hoping someone else will die. How true is that? That is exactly what had been in me all of these years, real poison, and my hoping my dad would die or at least suffer like we suffered because of him. So, I was ready (or so I thought) to really face this giant in my life, put this behind me, and hope he would want some kind of relationship and try to be some kind of dad.

Jimmy and I went on a mission to find him, and we did. We went on a week-long trip to Kentucky, and after all these years I was able to tell my biological father that I forgave him. He never really admitted anything, he just said, "I am sorry I hurt you." During that same week, I found out I had a nine-year-old half-sister named Melissa, and a stepsister named Glenda. We had a pretty good week, with many emotional ups and downs.

I really thought when we left Kentucky that week, my dad wanted to build a relationship with me and work toward seeing Daniel and Mark. Well, that never happened! I never saw my dad again. We talked a couple of times after that, but he never tried to do anything a dad should do. I was **so** disappointed and angry again. I eventually had to forgive him again and just move forward with the same ache and void in my life from not having a dad.

Many years went by, and one day, my brother Mark called me and said he found out on *geneology.com* that our dad had died about three years before. It didn't even really bother me. It was sad, but didn't really phase me. I was more concerned over why nobody let us know. I found out later from my sister, Melissa, that they tried to find us to tell us, but she didn't know my married last name, etc. Anyway, our father died of a brain aneurysm and he had at least three heart attacks before that. I haven't seen my sister since she was nine years old. She is now in her early thirties, has two boys, and is pregnant now with a little girl. We talk through Facebook now, but I do hope to see her again one day.

Later in life, God did put a man in my life who I felt comfortable enough with to call Dad. I will always thank God for David Harper. We had a special relationship, and

I loved talking with him, drinking hot tea with him, and laughing with him. We were really close. He helped me through many hard times, and just helped fill that dad void for about ten years. Then he died of cancer, but his legacy lives on through his children and grandchildren to this day.

CHAPTER FIVE

INFERTILE TO ADOPTION

GOD IS FAITHFUL

Isaiah 40:31 – *"But those who wait on the Lord Shall renew their strength; They shall mount up with wings like eagles, They shall run and not be weary, They shall walk and not faint."*

DURING MY WHOLE CHILDHOOD, PEOPLE WOULD ask me what I wanted to be when I grew up. I really didn't know what career I wanted, but I my answer was always, "All I want to be is a good wife, and a good mom."

I had very heavy and painful menstrual cycles ever since I started my period when I was nine years old. They were so bad, sometimes I would pass out from pain, and be on prescription strength pain medicine to help me through them. Jimmy and I tried for years to have kids, and I never could get pregnant. We went to the doctor, and after many tests, I found out I had severe endometriosis all over my uterus, so it would be impossible for me to have children. This was devastating news to me. I went into a deep depression. I could barely handle going to stores and seeing moms with their children, and thinking I would never know the joy of being a mom. All my dreams were shattered, and I just felt like a zombie walking around the world, not fully alive at all. I was a robot that just went to work, helped take care of things at home, and tried to be a good wife to Jimmy. All the while, I truly felt like death warmed over. All the joy I knew God had given me was not there. I tried to muster up a happy face and put on a smile, and say, "I'm fine" when people shook my hand and asked how I was doing. Parts of me screamed and just wanted to say, "**I am not fine**, and **I need help!**" I was trying to be the strong Christian woman people knew me to be, but I felt so alone.

Jimmy and I were really having a lot of problems. He was depressed because he was hurt and couldn't work, and now we had this news. He knew I was not doing good emotionally. One day we decided together that we really wanted to be parents and were going to start the foster to adopt classes to become foster parents. We had high hopes of being able to adopt one day. We were very excited about this, but people around us were not that excited.

They were full of questions and doubts. That was disappointing to us, and we didn't understand why. I think they just didn't want us to get hurt by the system. I of all people sure didn't want to be hurt by the foster care system either, but we wanted to rescue a child or two. At first, we wanted a baby, so hopefully they wouldn't have too much to heal from before finding their forever family.

So, we went through the foster care classes, home inspections, paperwork, etc., to become foster parents in Georgia. Shortly after we finished our classes, we got a phone call from one the social workers who said, "We have two children that really need a home, they are brother and sister, ten and seven years old, and if you don't take them, they will be separated next week." We immediately said yes, we wanted them, and agreed to meet them. Wow, that day changed our lives forever!

I won't go into all of the details here, but finally we got to bring James and Jessica home on November 17, 2006. James was ten and Jessica had just turned seven. They had been through a lot and witnessed a lot in their young lives. They had suffered a lot of hurt, fear, neglect, and they had lived in eight other homes before coming to our house. Jimmy and I had no idea what we were in for, or the challenge it really was going to be. The night they came to our house, we got them with only the clothes on their backs and nothing else. We went shopping the next day, and literally had to get everything, and spent over $1,000 in clothes, bedroom stuff, school supplies, some toys, and just everything two kids would need.

They were both full of fear, anger, hurt, bitterness, and rage. We had them both for six months. Due to some issues that came up with James, the social workers and judge decided to separate them, and James went to another home. We still saw him once a year at Christmas time, when Jessica's biological family got together. It was one of the hardest things for me for them to be separated, because I knew all too well the pain of that. At the same time, I knew it was best for this situation. I still loved James, and I still do to this day, and hope he always knows that.

After a while, we settled into our new normal, and thought we were going to be the happy little family...finally. On December 9, 2008, our adoption of Jessica was official. I can still hear her running around saying, "I got a new name, I got a new name!" We changed her middle name to my name, Elisabeth, so now she was Jessica Elisabeth. I won't state my previous last name, to protect certain things in our lives now. We had an adoption celebration at Golden Corral with our family and friends. Finally, I was a wife and a momma.

Many times during this whole adoption process, it would have been easy to give up, because we faced many challenges. Our love for Jessica, and wanting to protect her, kept us going. I am **so** glad we did. God taught me a lot about His faithfulness during this time.

If you are reading this and have dreams in your life that haven't been fulfilled yet, please hold on and know that God is faithful. He will give you the desires of your heart as long as they line up with His will for your life.

CHAPTER SIX

WALKING ON EGGSHELLS

GOD AS MY COMFORTER

Psalm 57:1- *"Be merciful to me, O god, be merciful to me! For my soul trusts in You; And in the shadow of Your wings I will make my refuge, Until these calamities have passed by."*

JIMMY, JESSICA, AND I LIVED ABOUT ONE "HAPPY" year together, before the bottom fell out, as people would say. I worked full-time in Atlanta as a legal billing specialist. Jimmy couldn't work because of his neuropathy and other health issues, so he stayed home with Jessica and did some things around the house. Let me just say that was very hard for me, but I knew I had to provide for us. Jimmy did get a disability check, but it wasn't very much.

I was still very thankful for family and did all I could to be a good wife and good mom.

Diabetes and neuropathy really took over Jimmy's life and he lived in so much pain. He would cry from his feet and legs hurting. I remember many nights waking up, and he would be in the shower with steaming hot water running on his feet and legs, trying to numb the pain. Jimmy was a heavy man, and was on some pain medications, but they never seemed to really work. His pain grew worse and worse, and so did his temper. I'm not going to go into all of the details, but I will give you enough to get some perspective of what our life was like for years. We lived our lives walking on eggshells, never knowing what to expect day to day, and sometimes minute to minute.

Jimmy got hooked on major narcotics and became a monster who terrified Jessica and me. We did our best to stay away from home as much as possible, because we never knew what kind of mood he was going to be in. I mean, we could have a great morning, go to church, and come back home to hell on earth. He was taking so many pills, he could barely stay awake some days. He would have hallucinations and be drawing in the air with his hands. I did my very best to have people help me watch Jessica, so she didn't have to be alone at home with him. However, there were too many times where she had to be home with him, and I still feel bad about that. At the same time, I had to keep my job. I kept Jessica as busy as I could with sports and church events, to help her escape our home life. People had no idea what we were going through. He would just snap at us for any little reason or start throwing stuff at us. I really didn't know how to get out. I felt trapped, and really didn't have any help. There wasn't anyone we could stay with for a long period of time. We did leave for a few days at a time, and go back, because he had a lot of medical problems that I had to help with.

At the same time, he wouldn't stop eating up all of our food. I only had a certain amount of money to go to the store each week and did my best to stretch the money. It got to a point where I was having to hide food at my job and take it back home each day so we could eat that day, or go to the store daily, and only buy what we would eat each day. Many times we were left with just ramen noodles to eat for a couple of days until I got paid again, because Jimmy had eaten everything else. Many times, I put bills off so we could have food. I had to rob Peter to pay Paul, if you know what I mean. My anger and frustration with him was growing daily.

I felt so bad for Jessica because she had already been through enough and didn't deserve to live like this. I thought I had to stay with him because it was the "right" thing to do.

Eventually, Jimmy's neuropathy got so bad in his feet that he lost one of his legs to diabetes. He was now in a wheelchair. Guess who had to lift this big wheelchair in and out of our car and push him around? That would be me. I did this for a few years.

Many times, we would be driving down the road with Jessica in the back seat and he would just start hollering and cussing at me for no reason. I knew Jessica was scared and so was I. I did my best to not say anything back, because I didn't want to make the situation worse. I would just look back at Jessica and have tears going down my face. I can't count the times we would be at home after dinner and he would go into one of his rampages. Then I would write Jessica a note, saying, "Go to the car, don't say anything, I will be right out." Then after I knew she was safely in the car, I would tell him we were going out for a while. We would stay out as long as possible to avoid going home. I know people wondered why we were hardly ever home, or why we were always the ones to go visit family. They had no idea the real hell we lived in. They thought they knew, but really only Jessica and I knew how bad all of that really was.

Have you ever wished someone would die, or pray for them to die? Well, that was me. I feel bad for even admitting that, but truly I began to hate him. Yet I was trying to love him at the same time. I kept thinking he would see God in me and want to change and get help. That didn't happen until later. You will see that in a couple of chapters.

Jimmy had many health problems, such as diabetes and high blood pressure. A blood clot went to his lungs and he was in the ICU for a long time. Many diabetes-related issues really should have taken him out of this world, and each time I would think, *This is it, this has to be it.* Then I would have been faithful to my vows and stuck by him through everything until death do us part. You know, the "Christian" thing to do.

During these really hard years, God did send people to help us pay some bills or give us money to do something fun. I did my best to make good memories with Jessica even through all of the hard times. We have a lot of funny stories, and I thank God for Him giving her to me. I thank God for the many friends and family who did try to help us as much as they could. People would tell me to leave him, but didn't really have any real suggestions for where to go or how we were going to leave and be able to make it. So, leaving wasn't a real solution.

Many nights I would go to bed crying my eyes out and begging God to change our situation. God filled me with scripture and different songs to help me worship, and literally carried me through this time. One of the songs He gave to me and Jessica is, *Worship While I'm Waiting*, by John Waller (https://youtu.be/3gjXBMC8-oM). That became our theme song, and almost every time we would get in the car, that song would come on the radio. Jessica and I would just belt it out, going down the road, and knew that was our prayer to help us worship while were waiting for our nightmare to be over.

Chapter Seven

Worst Nightmare

God as my counselor

Jeremiah 29:11 *"For I know the thoughts that I think toward you, says the Lord, thoughts of peace and not of evil, to give you a future and a hope."*

THIS WAS PROBABLY THE HARDEST CHAPTER I HAD to write. Due to the circumstances of this situation, I can't go into a lot of details. I can share enough for you to get the gist of what happened, and how hard this time in our life was. Before we started the foster to adopt process, people would tell us, "Be sure you get a baby because you never know what an older child has been through and will accuse you of." We didn't listen to them, and just thought they were trying to put doubts in our minds.

I will never forget, shortly after the adoption was final-ized, when Jessica was nine years old. We were driving down the road and she said, "Mommy, I need to tell you something, but I don't know if you will believe me."

I think my heart sank to my stomach, and I had no idea what she was about to say, but I knew it was serious. I pulled over, and the next few minutes changed our lives forever.

I said, "What is it, Sweetie?"

In her tiny voice she said, "Daddy is touching me in bad places."

I was thinking, *Nooo this can't be happening in my house, history can't be repeating itself!* I asked her to explain what she meant and what happened. Of course, I can't and won't go into details about any of that. Something about what she was saying rang true to me, and I was just shocked, confused, angry, devastated.

I told Jessica I would take care of it and would talk to Jimmy about it. He had never been accused of anything like this. I knew Jessica had been through a lot before she came to us, and I didn't know if she was just angry with him for his anger toward us, and trying to get him out of the house. So many questions come to mind when faced with a situation like this.

That evening, I confronted Jimmy with what Jessica said. He acted surprised and said he was just tickling her and she must have misunderstood it. We called Jessica into the living room, and Jimmy began apologizing for making her feel uncomfortable, and explaining he was just playing around with her. Jessica didn't say anything, and this situation went away for a little while. I was thinking she had to have just misunderstood what happened and took his tickling as something else.

After that night, it seemed like Jimmy's anger and temper with Jessica was even worse than before. I didn't know if he was feeling worse, or what the problem was, but he took everything out on her. Again, I did my best to not have her be home alone with him very often, but sometimes it was impossible to keep her away, and I had to work. I know Jessica played outside a lot and would wait for me to come home most days to come back inside (I didn't blame her).

Then one night when Jessica was ten years old, I was putting her to bed and she started crying really bad. I didn't know what was wrong.

She said, "I remember every detail, and I feel so gross!"

I asked her what she was talking about, and what details she remembered. I thought she was talking about something that happened to her before she came to us. Then she continued telling me some disgusting details of some things she said Jimmy did to her, but she didn't want to lose our family. You talk about a momma bear coming out. Also I was freaking out inside. *Like, what the hell is going on?* First, I confronted Jimmy with this new allegation, and of course he denied it totally. He was saying all kinds of things, telling me Jessica was sick and must have put his face on someone else who did this to her. Jessica was adamant it was him. I didn't know who to believe or what to do. I knew I had to protect her, and was scared for what all of this meant. *What if it is true? How could this happen in my house?*

I asked Jimmy to leave the house, telling him I couldn't deal with this and not knowing the truth. He stormed off and went to his brother's house. I called the police, and a detective came out. They questioned Jessica, and then went to question Jimmy. There wasn't any evidence of anything. What she said he did, there wouldn't be evidence, but it was disgusting and very wrong. Again, I felt in my heart she was telling the truth. I didn't want to believe it, that my husband could do something like that. The police didn't do anything. They said there was no evidence of anything, and we needed to work things out.

When we told his and some of my family what was said, they didn't believe Jessica at all. They totally turned against her and told me I needed to send her back, and there was no way he could ever do something like that! I can't even describe the rejection and betrayal Jessica went through during this time. I was pretty much the only one there for her. My brother, Daniel was in support of her, too, but he lived in Augusta and couldn't do much from there. Other than that, everyone else turned on her and said she was lying. Jessica and I even had to leave our home church, because we didn't want everyone asking us questions about where Jimmy was all of the time. We dealt with it for a long time, but we always had to lie to them and just say he wasn't feeling good or something. It became too hard to keep dealing with the questions and carrying this heavy load and not be able to talk about it. We loved our church. Leaving was one of the hardest things I ever had to decide to do, but I had to help and protect Jessica.

Jimmy lived in his brother and sister-in-law's basement for a couple of months while we all went to some counseling. We had a counselor coming to talk with all of us, trying to get to the bottom of it, and why Jimmy was so angry. Jessica was having a hard time emotionally and at school. I was falling apart on the inside, but still had to work. Jessica was involved in sports at this time, and thankfully could stay after school for practice most of the time until I got off work. Other times, she would go to her cousin's house. During all of this, Jimmy was still calling us every day and wanting to come home. Jessica would talk to him sometimes.

I heard him ask her one time, "Jessica, can you tell Mommy that didn't happen?"

She just handed me the phone back and didn't say anything. I don't think she knew I heard him ask her that question.

I called some dear friends who lead a forgiveness ministry; to see if they would be willing to meet with us to work through some issues and forgiveness. I told her what was going on in our home, and how confused I was. I had a "he said/she said" serious situation going on, and had no idea what was the right thing to do. I was a Christian wife with a disabled husband, and now a daughter who was hurting deeply and accusing him of the most awful things. I really felt like I was going crazy as they both stood their ground, insisting they were telling the truth.

My friend and her husband agreed to have us to come over and talk with them. I am sure they weren't prepared for everything that took place that day. We ended up being there a total of ten hours. Jimmy and I went first and talked about many issues, and forgave each other for a lot in our marriage. In the middle of us talking Jessica called me from school, and said she was sick; not throw up sick, just didn't feel good. I asked my friend if I could leave and pick her up from school. My friend thought it might be that Jessica was just nervous about everything we would be talking about.

She said, "Sure, go get her and bring her back here, and we will talk with her too."

Long story short, Jessica talked with my friend and told her the same details she had told me. However, my friend's husband had spent most of the day with Jimmy and talking with him. He said there was no way Jimmy was capable of doing what Jessica said he did. I saw Jessica just sit there with a pale face and very little visible emotion. She always had a hard time expressing her emotions anyways, so I wasn't surprised by that. My friend thought it was odd that Jessica didn't have any emotion, and thought Jessica was just really angry with Jimmy for the way he was treating us, and wanted him out of the house. Even though my friend felt this way, she led Jessica through forgiveness as if this really happened.

One of the steps in the process, at the end of the prayer, is praying a blessing over the person you are forgiving. I will never forget that Jessica prayed for Jimmy to be able to get a pair of shoes. He didn't have any shoes that fit him, because his feet were so swollen, and he walked around with only socks on. My heart about burst apart when I heard the sweetest, most genuine prayer come from her heart for her daddy.

Jessica knew our friends didn't believe her, but she never spoke up. I believe to this day she just wanted her family back and was willing to let everything go to make it happen. After all of us crying and praying together, we decided Jimmy should come back home.

Oh boy, here we go! For a little while, things were a lot better than they ever were. We went on picnics, and Jimmy took Jessica mudding in his truck. The accusations and lack of support were always in the back of my mind, but I didn't have a way of getting to the truth and getting peace about anything.

Then Jimmy's old ways started coming out again, and his pain was terrible. His anger, temper, and pill addiction were terrible again. I was at my wits' end and really didn't think I could take it anymore. Jimmy was having terrible headaches. He was supposed to be the one to pick up Jessica from school, as I still worked in Atlanta. I can't count the times Jessica would call me and tell me that Daddy didn't show up to pick her up. I hated for that to happen to her, and I worried every day at work if he was going to get up to go get her. She had a scholarship to go to a private school, so there wasn't a bus that she could ride to bring her home during this time. Thank God for my brother-in-law, Darrell, whom I loved so much. He worked in heating and air, and he knew our situation, and felt terrible for us. He always told me he would help us in any way he could, and did many times. On the days Jimmy didn't show up to pick up Jessica, we would call Darrell, and he would leave whatever he was doing to go pick her up.

Jessica turned eleven years old, and wished she didn't. You may remember in my childhood story that eleven was a terrible age for me as well. There is a country song *11* by Cassadee Pope (https://youtu.be/UeU2d9Mjui8) that says, "I wish I never turned eleven!" Jessica and I both relate to that song very much. We lived in a trailer behind the home of people we called Papa and MawMaw during this time. I will never forget one evening when I came home from work, Jessica was over at Mawmaw's house, and Jimmy was at our house. Jessica called me and asked me to come to Mawmaw's house that she needed to tell me something. She started telling me the worst thing I could imagine about something terrible Jimmy did to her that day. There was no way she made it up. There were details about what she said that I knew were true, and rage ran through me. Oh, my goodness! Was she really telling the truth the whole time, and I brought this monster back home? I brought Jessica back home, because I wanted her to be there when I confronted Jimmy with what she was accusing him of. I wanted to see how they reacted to each other, so I could try to figure out who was telling the truth. He of course denied it totally.

Jessica yelled at him, saying, "Yes, you did do that to me, and you know it!"

Now this was a tiny eleven-year-old girl standing up to a huge man she was already afraid of. I knew in my heart from the details she gave me and her courage in standing up to him that she was telling the truth.

By this time, Jimmy had already lost his leg and was in the wheelchair. He rolled down the ramp and went and barricaded himself in the tool shed. He called me, telling me he was going to kill himself. Jessica and I went to Papa and MawMaw's house and told them everything that happened. All they could do was cry with us. Mawmaw called Jimmy's dad (who lived across the street at this time) and told him his son was in the tool shed, threatening to kill himself. I called the police again, and again the police came out. They interviewed Jessica and Jimmy and didn't know who to believe, because again there was no evidence of anything. This time I was done, totally done with this situation ever coming up again.

I made Jimmy leave, and he went to live with his brother again. He eventually got his own trailer in the same neighborhood as us. Jimmy never came back to live with us, and you will learn in the next chapter how this all ended.

During this time, Jessica and I pretty much became nomads. Seriously, we moved so much I can't even count how many times we moved. Many situations came up, and things happened that caused us to have to move, way too often. Remember, I was used to having Jimmy's disability check, and it came to a screeching halt when he had to move out and get his own place. That made it even harder on me financially.

I look back at this time in our lives and wonder how in the world we made it. God made it possible. Through the help of some friends, and family, and of course me working myself to death, we made it! Praise the Lord, we made it to the other side of this nightmare.

CHAPTER EIGHT

OUTSIDE PRISION WALLS

GOD AS MY DEFENDER

2 Corinthians 4:8-9 *"We are hard pressed on every side, yet not crushed; we are perplexed, but no in despair; persecuted, but not forsaken; struck down, but not destroyed."*

IN MY HEART, I KNEW WHAT JESSICA WAS SAYING was true, but I never thought we would see the day that Jimmy confessed. After all, he had lied and lied, and caused his family and some of my family to reject Jessica. We used to be able to go to the houses of people we thought were family and friend, who had kids, so Jessica could play. Once this accusation came out, that stopped. People thought Jessica was lying and didn't want anyone in their houses to be accused. So, what was already a hard situation became even harder and very lonely for both Jessica and me.

Jimmy was drinking heavily and taking pain pills to the point of almost passing out. He was calling and begging us to come spend some time with him and let him throw the softball with Jessica. Sometimes, we did and tried to have some kind of relationship. We just didn't know how to move on. I can't describe well enough how painful this whole situation was for all of us.

Jessica was fourteen years old by this time. We went to the house of one of our friends to help pray for our friend, Kimmie, who was dying of brain cancer. During the time we were there, the lady friend of mine who leads the forgiveness ministry was also there. She told a story, and at the end of it she said, "Sometimes, you have to give people **one** more chance to tell the truth." That is the only sentence of her story I can remember now.

At the same moment, Jessica and I looked at each other and agreed we had to go confront Jimmy **one** more time and give him **one** more chance to tell the truth. We left our friend's house and headed over to confront Jimmy. I had no idea how this was going to go, but it was important to Jessica, so we went.

I will never forget this day as long as I live. We went in Jimmy's trailer, and Jessica said, "Daddy, I am here to give you **one** last chance to tell Mommy the truth about what you did to me! If you don't tell her the truth right now, I will never talk to you again!"

I was thinking, *Wow, she is so brave!*

Jimmy hung his head and rolled himself outside on the porch to smoke. He came back in the trailer with tears in his eyes, and looked at me and said, "Yes, it is true! Everything Jessica said I did is true, and I am so sorry!"

There was a sharp knife on his counter, and at that moment all I saw was red! ***What did you just say?*** In my mind and heart, I wanted to kill him. The only thing that kept me from stabbing him was God, and knowing Jessica still needed a mom. We all cried and cried, and I screamed and screamed! What I had thought was true in my heart had just been confirmed for sure. How could he possibly have brought himself to do that to her? He knew what she had already been through, how my abuse affected me as a woman, and caused so much hurt and rejection in Jessica's young life, and yet he did it anyway.

I told him he had to call of his family, the preacher, his counselor, and everyone he had lied to for all of these years, and tell them the truth. I sat there and listened to him make all of these phone calls and I told him he also had to turn himself in. The next day, my mom, my brother Mark, Jimmy's counselor, Jimmy and I went to the Henry County Police Department. Jimmy told them everything, he and his counselor went back with the investigator, and Jimmy had to write it all down. I got to read what he wrote, and it was exactly what Jessica said happened. I wanted to puke, and was so angry, hurt, and disgusted. The police department sent Jimmy back home. They said it would take about two weeks before a warrant would be issued, and then they would come to arrest him. I still can't believe they actually sent him back home for two weeks. I really thought he would kill himself during those long two weeks.

Jessica and I had moved in an apartment with my mom, and we were unpacking when the phone rang. A policeman on the other end of the line said, "I am here at Jimmy's house to pick him up, but since he is a bigger man with one leg, we can't get him in the back of the patrol car, and we need help getting him and the wheelchair to the jail. Will you please come take him to jail, and we will follow behind you? If you don't, then we will have to call a large van to come from Atlanta to help us get him to the jail."

So, of course, I said I would help. I had no idea how this was going to go, or how I was going to bring myself to do this.

God gave me the strength and peace I needed the whole way going to the jail. Jimmy and I didn't say a word to each other. Both of us had tears going down our faces, and I held his hand on the way there. Only God helped me do that. Even though I was angry and knew he needed to be punished for what he did, part of me was still scared for him and what he was about to face. Pedophiles don't normally fare too well in jail or prison, and there Jimmy was with one leg.

When Jimmy first went to the jail, and because he was so doped up, he was in the detox section for at least two months. I didn't hear from him or anyone at the jail for a long time. I don't know if you have ever known anyone in jail or prison, but let me tell you, the jail system is terrible. They have no communication skills, and nobody tells you anything you need to know if you have a family member in there. I didn't know he was going to need money to put on his account, or store as they call it. Finally, after about three months, Jimmy called me. He sounded terrible as he told me the things he needed. I had never been inside a jail or anything like that.

Jimmy was supposed to only be at that jail for three months before his hearing, but he ended up being there for six months. I went to see him a couple of times there, and then he had the court hearing where he would be sentenced. Jessica and I were there and actually got to talk to judge in the courtroom in front of everyone, with Jimmy sitting right there. The prosecutor told the judge all the details, and the judge read Jessica and my statements. He was going to give Jimmy forty years in prison with no chance of parole, but he asked if we wanted to say anything, and we did.

Only God could have given me and Jessica the strength to stand there that day and tell the judge what we did. We didn't want Jimmy to get that long of a sentence because he was already not doing very well physically, and we were working through forgiveness. We didn't want the bitterness and hate to continue to grow inside of us anymore. I believe the judge was in shock as we tried to express ourselves the best we could. Yes, Jimmy needed to be punished for what he did, but we knew he would never survive forty years in prison. The song, *Mercy Walked In*, by Gordon Mote (https://youtu.be/ShVKTFS4CSs), kept running through my mind. All I could think of was how God saw my sin, too, how He had mercy on me, and how I wanted to show that same mercy to others. Like I said earlier, it took a lot of work in my heart to go from wanting to kill Jimmy to having some compassion and mercy on him too. It was truly a war in my heart, spirit, and mind. The judge ended up sentencing Jimmy to twenty years, with ten years to serve in prison and ten out on probation. At the time of this writing, he was serving his sixth year in prison, and on dialysis.

Jimmy was transferred to Jackson State Prison, one of the deadliest prisons in Georgia. Every prisoner has to start off there, but are only supposed to be there a few weeks before they are sent to the prison where they will serve most of their time. However, with Jimmy only having one leg and other health issues, and the reason he was there, it took eight months before he finally went to the prison where he has been serving his sentence. In the Jackson State Prison, he saw many people killed, raped and beaten.

The first time I went to see him at the other prison (which I will not name), I was scared to death! The barbed wire fences, guards, security clearance to get in, and all of the different things you have to go through when you are there to see someone are a lot to process by yourself. I wasn't prepared for all of that, but I knew his family wouldn't come see him much. I am still to this day the only person in the outside world he can call. His family won't get a phone account so he can call them. I don't talk to him much at all anymore. I am thankful God took away the major rage, bitterness, and hate I had for him. I hope he does make it to get out and start a new life somewhere.

The pain of all of this is still very real, and there are still good days and bad days. We forgive, but we don't forget!

CHAPTER NINE

GOD IS IN THE DETAILS

GOD AS MY PROVIDER

Romans 8:28 -*"And we know that all things work together for good to those who love God, to those who are the called according to His purpose."*

THERE ARE SO MANY DIFFERENT STORIES I COULD share with you about how I have seen God's provision over and over in my life. I want to share with you a few that really stand out, as I watched God take care of me and Jessica during some really hard, dark times.

I have been a part of a women's ministry called Touching Hearts for the last 15 years. These women have walked along side me, supported me, and encouraged me through many dark times. A few years ago, we did a study on prayer and learned the importance of praying specifically for things in our lives. Yes, we pray, "Lord, thank You for this day, please bless my family, and keep us safe," and general prayers like that, but I had never really prayed for specific things in detail. I am not saying God is like some kind of genie in a bottle, who will grant any wish we make. I have learned over the last few years just how much God knows every single detail in our lives, how much He truly loves us, and how much He loves for us to talk to Him. So, I decided to try this new way of praying I had learned about and apply it to a few of our needs.

I have worked in Atlanta for the past twenty years, and when it gets cold, it is bitterly cold, with the wind blowing in between the high towers. I was riding the bus to and from work for a long time, freezing to death because I didn't have a coat. I honestly didn't have the money to get one. However, I didn't tell anyone I really needed a coat to deal with the extreme cold and wind while standing outside, waiting for a bus. One night I asked Jessica if she would pray with me that God would provide a coat for me. This way, we could both learn this important lesson about prayer, and her faith would grow as well as mine. We prayed every night for God to provide a coat. We knew He saw me out there, freezing, and that at the time we didn't have the money to get a coat.

I believe we prayed for a coat for three to five days. Then one day I was in the bathroom at work, washing my hands next to a lady I didn't really know that well.

All of a sudden, she said, "Do you need a coat?"

Oh my goodness, I think my jaw hit the sink. I wanted to scream **"Yes!"** I had tears in my eyes, and I said, "Yes, I do need a coat really bad."

She told me about this coat she was about to give to Goodwill, that she thought would fit me. I told her I didn't care what it looked like, if it had holes in it or whatever, I just needed something to stay warm. She said, "Okay, I will bring it to you tomorrow."

The next day, she brought me this awesome leather coat that was exactly my size. I couldn't wait to get home to show Jessica what God had done, providing the perfect coat for me. I also heard God telling me through this, *See, Elisabeth, I do see you and I'm not giving you a coat with holes in it, I am giving You my best!*

I believe that was the first time in my whole life that I truly felt God really loved me, Elisabeth. Not just that He died for the whole world or loved the whole world, but He really cared and love **me**! I am in tears just writing about this again.

Another time, someone paid for Jessica to go to a summer camp for two weeks. I was so thankful she was able to go and get a break. I also didn't want her to see how badly we were struggling at this time with food. I didn't care if I only ate one time a day, or whatever I needed to do, but I didn't want her to go through that with me. At this particular time, we were badly struggling financially, and I didn't let anyone know just how bad things really were. I felt like a burden to everyone, and feared they were tired of us always needing help. I also knew people knew our situation with Jimmy wasn't good, how he would eat up all our food for the week within two or three days, and then we would struggle to make it until my next payday.

Around 9:30 one night, I was just praying and telling God how much we needed food. We really were down to one can of green beans, and that was all we had in the house. I was quoting scripture, and I remember saying, "Lord, Your word says You would never see Your seed begging for food, and I am Your seed and I am begging for You to provide a miracle! I trust You and believe You will take care of us. Thank You that Jessica is gone to camp during this time." I just finished my prayer and didn't really know what we were going to do.

Around 10:00 that night, one my friends from church called me and said, "God has laid you on my heart, and I am calling to see if y'all need anything?"

I just started crying! I said, "Yes, we desperately need food, we are out of everything!" At this time, I hadn't talked much to this lady, and I hadn't shared our struggles, so I knew **only God** could have told her to call me. I really thought she would just bring us a few meals and I would be so thankful for whatever she did. The next day, she came to our house and looked in our pantry and refrigerator, and saw for herself that we literally had nothing. She took me to a couple of stores to stock up on food, cleaning supplies, and anything else we needed. I believe she spent $500 and our refrigerator and pantry were completely full. I thanked her and thanked her. I still haven't been able to pay her back, but she never asked for it back, she did it out of love and obeyed God.

I could go on and on with different stories about how God has provided and taken care of us. I appreciate everyone who helped us make it in many different ways. I challenge you to start praying for specific things in your life, and watch God move. I believe God allowed me to see Him as my provider for many reasons. He knew I was going to really need strong faith for the next mountains I was about to face in my life.

CHAPTER TEN

LOOKING FOR LOVE

GOD AS MY VICTORY

Deuteronomy 20:3-4 *"Do not let your heart faint, do not be afraid, and do not tremble or be terrified because of them; for the Lord your God is He who goes with you, to fight for you against your enemies, to save you."*

AT THE TIME OF THIS PARTICULAR STORY, JIMMY had been in prison now for three years. Even before he was arrested, we hadn't lived together in two years, and I had felt pretty much alone for at least ten years. This left me feeling very desperate and lonely, and really wanting to experience real love. I felt like the third wheel everywhere I went. It was even hard to go to church because I would see all these couples and families who looked truly happy. Honestly, I was jealous. I had to continually pray for God to help me not be jealous, and just be content with what I had.

Don't get me wrong, I was more than thankful to have Jessica and be a mom to her. I was just miserable inside and wanted someone to love me for me.

At this same time, my closest brother-in-law, Darrell, was dying of cancer. Jessica was having a very hard time emotionally and making some bad decisions in her senior year. I won't go into that in this book, because that is part of her story that I believe one day she will share. I know Darrell meant a lot to Jessica too, and she didn't know how to deal with him dying either. We both still miss him very much today. He was really the only one of Jimmy's brothers who truly helped us, and accepted Jessica. I say all of this to lead up to what happened next in my life.

One day I was on Instagram and a private message came through from a person named "Larry Brown." I kept deleting his follow request, and then he said, "Hey, I just want to get to know you." I know now that I never should have even entertained the idea of responding to him. However, I just convinced myself...what would it hurt to have a "friend" in California? So, we began talking through Instagram, and then exchanged phone numbers. His picture was of a cute, older white man. He told me he was fifty-two, worked on an oil rig in California, and when he got off it, he wanted to come meet me in person.

This went on for six months. I truly had fallen in love with this "Larry Brown," and I couldn't wait to meet him. When I would tell people about him, they would just laugh at me and say, "I hope it works out." I guess they could see what I couldn't at that time. I wanted to prove them wrong, that this was real, and we were going to make it work.

He even convinced me to send him money through CashApp to help him get things he needed on the rig, and pay for phone calls to me. He helped me through many hard nights when Darrell was dying, and we were trying to be there for the rest of the family. "Larry" helped me through some hard times with different things going on at this time in my life.

The time came for me to finally meet "Larry Brown." We agreed I would pick him up from the airport. I got there and waited and waited for him to show up. He didn't come on the flight he was supposed to be on. I called him to see where he was.

He said, "I need you to go somewhere private so I can tell you something really important." My heart sank to my stomach, as I had no idea what he was about to say. He said, "How would you feel if I told you that my name is really Prince, I am black, I am thirty years old, and I live in Nigeria?" I think my heart stopped in that moment. I couldn't believe what I was hearing. He tried to convince me he loved me, and he was sorry he lied to me.

I really looked crazy for believing everything he had been telling me for six months. This shattered my already hurting heart. I didn't talk to him for a long time after that. Then finally one day we talked, and I told him to never call me again. I still can't believe how naïve I was. It shows just how desperate I was.

Through a series of events I can't go into here, we had to move again after Jessica graduated high school. She moved to Augusta, and I moved in with my mom. I was feeling very lonely and missing my daughter so much. Then another guy tried to do the same thing to me, but this time I caught him in all the lies within two months and ended that.

However, despite all this, I was still searching to find real love. I hadn't been touched or really loved by a man in over a decade. I was legally still married, but soon I started the divorce process. Finally our divorce was done, and I wasn't married to Jimmy anymore, but during this time I started spiraling downward into a deep, dark pit of depression. I didn't know how to get out of it. Even though I knew God loved me and had brought me through so much, I just felt like there was something wrong with me. Why couldn't I find anyone to really love me? I continued my search with different online dating sites. I met some real creepers, and most just wanted one thing.

I will not discuss many aspects of this part of my life in this book. If I am given the opportunity to share my story publicly someday, I will share more in person. Maybe I will go into more details with another hurting lady I meet, so she will know she isn't alone and that God loves her and forgives her, and she doesn't have to live in shame anymore.

My suggestion is to never trust anyone you can't meet in person within two weeks, or if they start asking you for money. Some things happened in this part of my life that I don't believe I will ever be fully over. They made it hard for me to trust anyone. A song that meant a lot to me during this time, when I felt totally shattered and broken, was, *Tell Your Heart to Beat Again*, by Danny Gokey (https:// youtu.be/F77v41jbOYs). My friend, if you are at the end of your rope please don't give up! Allow God to carry you through these times and let your heart beat again.

Thankfully, God has shown me His grace, mercy, and forgiveness. I can now talk about this time in my life without totally breaking down, and hope to use the things I have learned to help others.

CHAPTER ELEVEN

LIFE AND DEATH

GOD AS MY ONLY HOPE

Jude 1:24 – *"Now to Him who is able to keep you from stumbling, And to present you faultless before the presence of His glory with exceeding joy. "*

IN FEBRUARY 2018, MY DEPRESSION WAS DESCENDING to a really scary place. I was still trying to survive, but I felt worthless, like a failure, and dirty. I started having a lot of physical issues I couldn't explain. I wasn't sleeping much at all, and had severe burning sensations in my arms and hands. I went to many different doctors, trying to find out what was wrong with me. I ended up on some nerve pain medicine for neuropathy, but the medicine made me so drowsy, it was hard to drive or focus at work. Things got so bad over the next five months; I truly forgot how to do life. I forgot how to do my job and was making mistakes.

Then on July 30, 2018, I decided I didn't want to live this life anymore. I planned how I was going to kill myself that weekend. On July 30, I quit my job. The next day I turned my car in to the place I was making payments for a title loan because, "I wasn't going to need it anymore." I know my mom, daughter, and brothers were very concerned about me. To be honest, at this time I didn't care. Satan had convinced me I didn't deserve to live anymore, I would never find true happiness, and I was a burden to my mom and everyone around me.

I did try to cut myself deep enough that weekend to end it, but I couldn't go deep enough. From August to October 2018, I was constantly thinking of new ways I could try to die. I had cut out almost everyone in my life. I didn't want to get out of bed, didn't take a shower, and I forgot how to even shop at the grocery store. I would just go in and walk around like a zombie, and come out with very little. I know I looked terrible. My thyroid level was all over the place. Doctors were trying to help me, but nothing worked.

Near the end of October, my mom called my brother Daniel to come help take me to a mental hospital to see if they could help me. I knew she was afraid every day that I was going to succeed in trying to die. I won't say where I went, but it wasn't a good place at all. I know if my mom and brother knew what this place was really like, they wouldn't have put me there. I truly thought I was going to die in there, and never get out. This place was more for drug addicts. I saw things I will never forget, and was in there with some truly crazy people.

I was there for two weeks and finally got to go home because I wasn't responding to their treatment. Honestly, I fought everything they tried to do to me and all of the psychotic meds they tried to give me. Things happened in this hospital that I still don't understand *how* they happened. All I can say is, "**But God!**" He knew Satan was out to destroy and kill me, and **God** rescued me. There is **no** doubt in my mind there was a true spiritual battle of good and evil going on over my life. Thankfully, God won the war!

When I came home from the hospital, right before Thanksgiving of 2018, I still wasn't doing that good emotionally. I spent two weeks just crying out to God, singing/listening to worship songs, and quoting scripture **out loud**! That is something Martha, my friend, mentor and leader of Touching Hearts, taught me is to say scripture out loud because it would make the enemy flee. Satan is the prince of the air, and when we claim the blood of Jesus over us, he can't stand it.

I know from firsthand experience the battlefield truly is in the mind, and how important it is to take every thought captive. 2 Corinthians 10:3-5, *"For though we* *walk in the flesh, we do not war according to the flesh. ⁴ For the weapons of our warfare are not carnal but mighty in God for pulling down strongholds, ⁵ casting down arguments and every high thing that exalts itself against the knowledge of God, **bringing every thought into captivity** to the obedience of Christ."*

Even though I had no strength of my own, I didn't *feel* what I was saying at the time, and couldn't see how God was going to rescue me through this mess. Now I didn't have a job, or a car, and was a total mess. I felt so heavy and embarrassed about how bad this situation got. I didn't know how to help my mom, and I knew she was burnt out. Slowly, over two weeks, the heaviness started to lift, and I started to feel more like myself. I started to believe God truly forgave me, and loved me for who I am, and truly cared about my broken heart. There is a song by Natalie Grant called *Clean (https://youtu.be/Idm7RlwrZVw)*, that I just played and sang over and over, because it felt like my story and how I felt. I encourage you to listen to this song and truly listen to the words. Always remember there is nothing too dirty that God can't make worthy.

I am so thankful to be able to say that God truly has and still is restoring me piece by piece. I did get another job, and my mom got a new car, and gave me her older car. I started going back to church, and back to Touching Hearts which I missed so much! They welcomed me back

with open arms. That is how the body of Christ is supposed to be.

We never know what someone is going through, or
hiding behind the "I'm fine" smile. I pray for God to use
me to be a vessel He can use, a representation of His hands
and feet to this hurting world. The Bible tells us that the
world will know we are His by our love for each other.

> **John 13:35,** *"By this all will know that*
> *you are My disciples, if you have love for*
> *one another."*

After I was on the other side of this and I felt like God
was truly healing me, I wanted to get a tattoo of some
kind to be a conversation starter to help me share hope
with others. The picture of the butterfly with the word
Overcomer under that you see at the beginning of each new
chapter is actually a picture of my tattoo on my wrist. If
you notice, the body of the butterfly is a semicolon. The
semicolon tattoo stands for suicide/depression awareness.
Then the butterfly wings show the transformation that
God has done and is doing in my life. The word *Overcomer*
means a lot to me! The Bible talks a lot about us being
more than conquerors and how God helps us overcome
things in life. Here are two of my favorite verses that I
claim over my life, and hope you will too.

John 16:33, *"These things I have spoken to you, that in Me you may have peace. In the world you will have tribulation; but be of good cheer, I have **overcome** the world."*

Isn't that just so comforting to know and be reminded that nothing takes Him by surprise, and He truly has overcome the world!

Romans 8:37-39, *"Yet in all these things we are **more than conquerors** through Him who loved us. For I am persuaded that neither death nor life, nor angels nor principalities nor powers, nor things present nor things to come, nor height nor depth, nor any other created thing shall be able to separate us from the love of God which is Christ Jesus our Lord."*

Chapter Twelve

Precious Gift

God as my redeemer

Matthew 19:26 – *"But Jesus looked at them and said to them, "With men this is impossible, but with God all things are possible."*

I WAS DOING A LOT BETTER PHYSICALLY AND EMOtionally by January 2019. I was back in my reality of living with my mom, and helping my brother, Mark, and his kids through some very hard times. I was feeling very alone and really missing my daughter, Jessica, who still lived in Augusta. One of my friends told me I should put a profile on *Match.com.* My first instinct was to say, "No way." After what I went through with the two scammers, I really didn't trust anything online.

Despite that, I went ahead and made a profile on *Match. com*, and planning to be very cautious and see what happened. I still had a bad self-image of myself. Since I am a bigger woman, I really didn't think anyone would want me. Unfortunately, I did have a few dates, and ran into some real jerks when they realized I wasn't giving myself to them. It was very frustrating! My feeling was: *Aren't there any good men out here anymore that really want to get to know me for me?*

On January 27, 2019, I was in the last week of my subscription on *Match.com*, and I had two new matches. One was Steve Womble, and someone else. I prayed over both guys, and just said, "This is it. If these guys are jerks, I am done totally with online dating." I sent both of them a message that simply said, "Hello, how are you doing? I hope you are having a good day!" Steve Womble replied to me, and we began to chat online. He then asked for my phone number, and after day three of us talking, he asked me to go out on a date. We went to Outback Steakhouse and had a great time! We had a lot in common, and just really enjoyed being together.

I learned shortly after our first date that January 27, 2019, was also six years to the day that Steve's previous fiancé, Ashely, was killed in a car wreck. I felt so bad for him, and the loss and grief he experienced. I believe since we have both experienced extreme pain and loss, it helps us not to take each other for granted. We just truly cherish every day! February 14, 2019 (Valentine's Day), Steve asked me to be his girlfriend and for us to become an official couple. Of course, I said, "**Yes!**" I was ecstatic! We spent as much time as we could with each other, even though he lived in Dunwoody, GA, and I lived in Newnan, GA.

I slowly began to tell him about my life and some of what I had just been through. He was very tenderhearted, and I could tell he truly cared about me, and wanted to protect me. I didn't want to scare him off or overwhelm him with the trauma I had experienced, or the current drama in our family. At the same time, I had some more physical problems all of a sudden, and didn't feel good. I had some neurological problems, a hard time walking, extreme fatigue, my bladder and bowels had stopped working, headaches, and other medical problems. I really thought something very bad was wrong with me. I was admitted to Fayette Piedmont for a few days for them to run tests on me. They gave me so much medicine to enable me to use the bathroom, it unbalanced several of my vitamins and electrolytes. Steve stood right be me through all of this and we had only been dating for a short time. I was sent home on February 22, and told to go see a neurologist.

Then on the evening of February 24, 2019 (my mom's birthday), I stood up from the kitchen table and felt a terrible pain in my chest and shoulders. I told my mom, "Call 911. Call 911." At first, I think she thought I was just scared from everything that was going on, and then I grabbed the phone and called 911. The ambulance came. My blood pressure was very high, but my EKG looked okay. I was still in a lot of pain and feeling extreme pressure in my chest and shoulders. They took me to Newnan Piedmont Hospital. I was there for hours, taking many different medicines that didn't touch the pain. They gave me nitroglycerin, aspirin, and a lidocaine patch, and I was still in a lot of pain. I stayed all night.

A nurse came in and said, "Your EKG looks good, but your heart enzymes don't look good and your Troponin level keeps increasing, it is an eleven, and I need to call my specialist."

Finally, the cardiologist came in and listened to my heart, and saw my blood work. I will never forget when he said, "Oh my goodness, get her down to the OR right now, she is having a heart attack!"

I saw real fear on my mom's face, and I had no idea what I was about to be in for.

I had three major blockages; one 99 percent blocked, one 95 percent blocked, and one 80 percent blocked. I had three stents put in, and stayed in the hospital for two days. Steve was by my side the whole time. I really thought he was going to leave me. I even told him it was okay if he left me. I knew he already had lost Ashley, and now here I was sick. It truly broke my heart, for him and for me. Thankfully, he didn't listen to me.

For the first time, he said, "Elisabeth, I know you have been through a lot, and I already love you so much, and I am not going anywhere!"

That meant so much to me, and still does to this day!

I was sent home with a walker because I still couldn't walk very well, and was so weak. I can't even explain how weak I was and the help I truly needed. My mom and I had a hard relationship at this time, and she didn't think I needed as much help as I did. She wouldn't let Steve come to the house unless she was there. In fact, no one could come. I am sure she feels bad about this now, but it truly hurt me to the core. I could barely walk, and there I was by myself, trying to recover from a heart attack. I had many doctor appointments I needed to go to, and no idea how I was going to get to them. I couldn't ask Steve to come from Dunwoody to take me to all of these appointments.

Literally the day before I had my heart attack, I had met with a lady I barely knew at Touching Hearts, Debbie. She had written a book, and I met with her to discuss how she did it and get ideas for me writing a book. Our hearts and spirits connected so much that day. I got to share my story with her, and she asked me to come speak at her ministry, Women at The Well. God knew I needed Debbie in my life, I just had no idea how much.

Debbie had seen on Facebook that I had a heart attack, and she called me to see if she could do anything for me. I told her I needed some rides to different doctors. She stepped right up to the plate, and took me back and forth to many doctor appointments. We really enjoyed our time together, and I thank God for Debbie and our friendship.

Things continued to be very hard between me and my mom, and I moved out. I can say now that God has brought about forgiveness on both of our parts and our relationship is a lot better now. There are things we just don't talk about, and try to be there for each other as much as we can.

Steve and I were doing great in our relationship and began to talk about a future together. August 14, 2019, he asked me to marry him. I again said, **"Yes!"** The best *Yes* of my life! I can't describe in enough words how much I love this man. God has used him to show me the gentleness of a man, and I feel God's love for me through Steve. To keep our theme of the 14th being an important date for us, we decided to get married on November 14, 2019.

We were going to have a nice wedding, but because of some family issues, and finances, we decided to just elope. So, on November 14, 2019, we had a small, sweet ceremony in Dahlonega, GA, and stayed in a nice cabin in the mountains. It was very sweet, and one of the best days of my life.

I am proud to be Elisabeth Womble. We have a wonderful life together, and our home is filled with laughter and joy. I am so thankful for the support and encouragement he has given me throughout the process of writing this book. As you can imagine, there have been many hard days and nights through rehashing everything in my life. Steve has been right there to hold me and let me cry it out, and encourage me to keep going. It has definitely been another layer of healing, and I am thankful to be able to share my story.

I love you, Steve, and thank God for giving me such a precious gift when He gave me you!

CHAPTER
THIRTEEN

DELIVERED BY GRACE

GOD AS MY DELIVERER

Hebrews 4:12 –*"For the word of God is living and powerful, and sharper than any two-edged sword, piercing even to the division of soul and spirit, and of joints and marrow, and is a discerner of the thoughts and intents of the heart."*

SHORTLY AFTER MY HEART ATTACK IN FEBRUARY 2019, I met with two my dear friends and mentors, Peggy and Kathie. These two ladies and several others have been rocks for me throughout my adult life. Peggy and Kathie pray with ladies and help deliver them from different bondages and spiritual warfare in their lives. I hadn't even told them everything that happened with the two guys who really hurt and scammed me online, and other mistakes I made during that dark time of my life. Kathie felt a lot of physical problems were coming from spiritual warfare. At first, I was kind of scared to tell them everything that happened, just because I was embarrassed. I knew they loved me no matter what, and they still did even after I told them. Many people don't believe in demon possession or spiritual warfare. I have believed in it most of my life, because I watched my mom struggle with these issues, and was in counseling for a long time. However, this was the first time I really realized it in my own life.

We spent a few hours of praying, crying, and releasing a lot of different spirits that obviously were weighing me down, and making me sick, emotionally and physically. Deeper work needed to be done. Thankfully, Kathie knew a man who only dealt with deliverance issues. I won't say his name here in the book, but if you reach out to me, I can put you in touch with him. Kathie helped me get an appointment with him. To say I was scared is an understatement. I didn't really know what to expect.

Steve drove me to his house, and I spent all day there. I can truly say this day changed my life forever. It was a very hard and emotionally draining day, but also a day I can look back to and say that was the day I found true **freedom**! Many different spirits had taken a stronghold in my life. I had to be willing to go back through many painful events of my life and allow this man to help me literally cast out these spirits that probably had been there most of my life, and just grew deeper. I now know the real importance of putting on the whole armor of God every day.

Seriously, up unto this point, my life seemed like it was just one big traumatic event after another. I didn't know anyone else around who had experienced even half of what I had been through. People who have been close to me through my adult life have many times told me, "I don't know what God has in store for you, but it must be something really big to trust you to carry all of these different things," or "I have never met anyone who has been through as much as you and you continue to smile." Really I would hear these things and I would think, *If you saw on the inside, I am dying, and I am tired of God allowing all of these bad things. I don't want to be strong anymore!* I always wondered if my family was cursed or something, or what in the world was wrong with me. I now know that yes, I did have curses over me from generations of different sins before me that weren't broken or confessed.

I know this is a heavy subject and not everyone believes in it. I can tell you firsthand it is very real. The spirit realm we live in is very real. It is truly a battle of right and wrong, and evil and good. **1 Peter 5:8,** *"Be sober, be vigilant; because your adversary the devil walks about like a roaring lion, seeking whom he may devour,"* is **very true!** The enemy, Satan, really does know our weaknesses and knows what lies to tell us to get us down. This is one reason I titled this book, ***Grace to See: Living with the Enemy; my story of survival***. I wasn't only talking about the enemy being my dad, mom's depression, the foster care system, my ex-husband, etc., I was also talking about the real enemy, Satan. I have come too close to death because of him and his lies.

Praise the Lord, I now know the keys to true deliverance and freedom. I am willing to talk with and pray with anyone about this. I pray God will use me and my testimony to help other hurting people find this same deliverance, joy, and peace. It is true that we don't wrestle against flesh and blood, but against principalities, powers, and rulers of darkness; and that we must put on the whole armor of God daily. (Eph. 6:10-18)

CHAPTER FOURTEEN

HIDDEN TREASURES

GOD AS MY PEACE

Isaiah 26:3 – *"You will keep him perfect peace, Whose mind is stayed on You, because he trusts in You."*

AS I LOOK BACK OVER MY LIFE, AND THE DIFFERENT circumstances I had to overcome, I can see several different hidden treasures God gave me along the way. The number one treasure would be He gave me a huge heart of compassion and mercy for other people. I have to constantly give situations I know about to God, so I don't carry them as heavily as I used to. I used to try to fix everyone's problems, and help them as much as I possibly could, but I burnt out very fast, and I wasn't taking care of myself. I have now learned I can love people, pray with them, help them as tangibly as I can, but I can't save the whole world, or fix everyone's problems. He has made me a great listener, and I don't judge people for anything, because I know I could be right there with them if it wasn't for God's grace.

Another treasure He gave me is that I am probably one of the world's best packers and movers. I have had to move so much in my life, and survive off of very little, that I can help organize anything. I have helped many friends to organize, get rid of stuff, or have yard sales to get ready to move, etc. I am also very thrifty, and taught my daughter, Jessica, how to be thrifty as well. Jessica watched me make good deals, and I taught her how to save money, and take care of bills when she was a teenager.

I love so much helping people now in any way I can. My husband and I are starting a blessing bag ministry to help some homeless people in our area. Right now, we are just doing about six blessing bags a month, and hope to increase it as money allows. Depending on the season of the year, we will fill the bags with different items that people will need, a small Bible, and gift cards of maybe $5 or $10, so they can at least get a meal or something to drink. I will also try to talk with some of these homeless people and sharing the gospel, and God's love with them. I want them to know they are not alone, we see them, God sees them and loves them just the way they are. When I had my nervous breakdown a couple of years ago, I truly imagined myself being homeless, and standing on the side of the street with a sign begging for help. When I pass homeless people now (which is far too often), I am reminded of that time, and thankful that God rescued me from that dark pit.

Learning to pray specifically for different things in life, and praying out loud the word of God, is probably one of the most special treasures I have now. It doesn't mean all my prayers are answered the way I want them to be, or when I want them to be answered. It does mean I know God wants the best for us and He wants to give us the desires of our hearts. James 4:2 says, *"You have not because you do not ask."* I have learned to really ask the Lord for things, and to align my heart with His will. I encourage you to give it a try. Keep a journal, if possible, of different prayer requests, and the date He answered the prayer. You will be amazed at how much He really cares about every detail of our lives.

Also, I have learned to pray really believing and expecting God to answer my prayer. A mustard seed of faith can move mountains. He wants to know that we trust Him and believe He will answer our prayers. As it says in Romans 8:25-27, *"But if we hope for what we do not see, we eagerly wait for it with perseverance. Likewise the Spirit also helps in our weaknesses. For we do not know what we should pray for as we ought, but the Spirit Himself makes intercession for us with groanings which cannot be uttered. Now He who searches the hearts knows what the mind of the Spirit is because He makes intercession for the saints according to the will of God."* I believe it is very comforting to know the Holy Spirit intercedes for us, and makes our requests known to God. He will do that for you too, my friend.

Writing scripture on notecards and carrying them with me through the day to read helps me memorize scripture. Having scripture printed out and taped on your bathroom mirror, refrigerator, anywhere you will see it several times a day, will also help you keep God's word in front of you. Remember, the devil likes to tell us lies about ourselves, but if we have our weapon of the sword (God's word), we can fight these lies with truth.

One important treasure that helps me when I start feeling down, or hearing bad lies about myself, is replacing the lie with God's truth. I write down on one side of the paper the lie I believe, then on the other side of the paper counteract that lie with God's truth from His word.

Examples below:

Lie	Truth
I am not good enough	I am perfect in Christ – Hebrews 10:14
I am unwanted / don't belong	I have been adopted by God - 1 John 3:1
I am alone	I am never alone – Hebrews 13:5-6

There is nothing special about me	I have been chosen / set apart by God – 1 Peter 2:9-10
I am in bondage	I am free – 2 Corinthians 3-17

These are just a few examples of defeating darkness with light, expelling the lie with the truth. Say these truths out loud, because then the enemy, Satan will have to flee and leave you alone.

There are many other treasures that God has given me, but the last one I will mention in this book is true joy. God has filled me with His joy and laughter. I love to laugh now, and I like to make people laugh. Laughter is contagious. Joy is different than being happy. Happiness depends on the circumstances if a person is happy or not. Real joy doesn't depend on circumstances. It is a rest, a peace in knowing God is in control and I am not. No matter what happens, good or bad, we know it had to pass through God to get to us, and He will give us exactly what we need to make it through any circumstance. Sharing our joy and our testimonies with others helps strengthen their faith, too. Who wants to join me in doing our best to be the hands and feet of Jesus to this lost, hurting, and dying world?

CHAPTER FIFTEEN

FOLLOW MY DREAMS

GOD OF NEW BEGINNINGS

Revelation 21:5 – **"Then He who sat on the throne said, "Behold, I make all things new." And He said to me, "Write, for these words are true and faithful."**

AS YOU READ MY STORY, I DON'T WANT YOU THINK I have it all together or everything is perfect in my world now, because that isn't the case at all. I still have many struggles I am praying for God to help me overcome. I just now have new tools to fight the enemy that tries to destroy me and take my joy. I can relate to a lot of different types of people, and I pray God will use me to bring Him glory.

I am sure you are wondering how my daughter, Jessica, is doing now. She is doing a lot better. She lives in Augusta with her boyfriend, and they had their first baby in January of this year, so I am now a Nana and I love every minute of it! Jessica has come a long way, and I know she still needs more healing from things that have happened in her life. I believe in the right time, she will get that. I am so proud of the young woman she has become, and she is such a good little mommy to precious Ava! I have a close relationship with both of my brothers and their kids. My relationship with Mom is a lot better, now that we don't live together, and I love her very much.

As I wrote this book, I was thinking about the many people in the world who are hurting and who feel like giving up. If this is you or you know someone who is at the brink of giving up, please don't ever give up! There is help out there. You have to let someone know you are desperate, and really need help. I wanted to close this book with some helpful phone numbers and encouragement. Below are numbers for a suicide hotline, domestic abuse help, an addiction hotline, and help for homeless hotline numbers:

National Suicide Prevention Lifeline
– 1-800-273-8255

Statewide Domestic Violence Hotline – GCADV.org
– 1-800-334-2836

**Women's Resource Center to end Domestic Violence
– 404-688-9436**

**Substance Abuse / Addiction Hotline
– 1-888-815-2561**

**Atlanta Mission – help for the Homeless
– 404-566-6439**

People need to know there is real help out here, and that they aren't alone. I am praying for everyone who reads this book to realize through my story of redemption that anything is possible with God. He does love you just the way you are!

I truly believe that as we face different circumstances, we learn a new attribute of God in a very personal way. Until we face certain situations, we can know in our heads He is our provider, but when we see Him work things out that only He could do, we know it in our hearts. Throughout this book, at the top of each chapter I listed a different characteristic God has taught me personally. I pray the same for you, that you will know Him as your peace, your joy, your strength, your friend, your comforter, your hope, your provider, your father/husband, your defender, faithful and most of important as your Savior!

I would also like to encourage you to start journaling and writing about times you can look back in your life and see God's hand of protection, His love, and His faithfulness in your life. Where have you seen God bring you through some really hard times? What dreams do you have that you need God to give you wisdom, direction, and peace about? Make a list of prayer requests, then put the date God answered that prayer, and how He answered. Remember, it may not always be the way we want Him to answer, but He does answer. Keeping a journal helps by giving you something tangible go back to when you are in another hard time and can't understand what God is doing in your life, to remember and know He is faithful. He is who He says He is, and He will do what He says He will do!

As God opens doors, I hope to start speaking at different churches, women's events, really anywhere He wants me to. I want to share the message of hope that only He can give. You are an overcomer through Him! Let's go be His hands and feet to the hurting world around us. Let your light shine everywhere you go!

I am excited for whatever the next journey of life God has for me to begin!

SONG LYRIC EXCERPTS:

Waller, J. (2007) *While I'm Waiting,* on **The Blessing.**
Beach Street Records, Nashville, Tennessee. (https://
youtu.be/3gjXBMC8-oM)

Pope, C. (2013) *11,* on **Frame by Frame.** Universal
Musical Publishing Group, Nashville, Tennessee.
(https://youtu.be/UeU2d9Mjui8)

Mote, G. (2008) *Mercy Walked In,* on **Mercy Walked In.**
Daywind, Nashville, Tennessee. (https://youtu.be/
ShVKTFS4CSs)

Grant, N. (2015) *Clean,* on **Be One.** Curb
Records, Nashville, Tennessee. (*https://youtu.be/
Idm7RlwrZVw*)

Gokey, D. (2014) *Tell Your Heart to Beat Again,* on
Hope in Front of Me. Salem Publishing, Nashville,
Tennessee. (https://youtu.be/F77v41jbOYs)

About the Author

Elisabeth Womble

ELISABETH WOMBLE IS AN ACTIVE MEMBER OF Touching Hearts Ministries in Fayetteville, GA. Touching Hearts is a women's ministry that encourages, loves, and empowers women from all walks of life. She loves to help others, and God has given her great compassion and mercy for hurting people. Elisabeth aspires to be a mentor for young women as a national speaker and author. She is very excited about ministry opportunities God has in store and would love to be invited to share her testimony to your church, small group, or women's ministry.

She has been a legal billing specialist at law firms in Atlanta, GA for 15 years. She currently lives in Douglasville, GA, where she is a wife, mother, new Nana, and enjoying starting her life over in victory. Please feel free to contact Elisabeth at <u>ewomble1114@comcast.net</u> and/or write letters to the following address:

Elisabeth Womble
4780 Ashford Dunwoody Road, Suite 540
#256
Atlanta, GA 30338

CPSIA information can be obtained
at www.ICGtesting.com
Printed in the USA
LVHW010839280121
677609LV00006B/647

9 781632 219817